THE CHOCOLATE LOVERS GUIDE TO SELF CARE - ONE BITE AT A TIME

How a Box of Chocolates can improve your self care

Anne Goodridge

To Mum
Love and thanks

CONTENTS

INTRODUCTION

I started writing this during the lockdown in March 2020. I had begun writing before, but events have overtaken the writing, coronavirus is causing us to think about how we live our lives. Things we took as being regular and our norms have been turned on their head. In my opinion, making it all the more important to think about self-care, or to put it another way, to think about how we look after ourselves.

Working from home is for some the new norm, many are worried about their employment, and children have missed school for several months and school bubbles are now a fixture. There is a lot for us all to get used. Even when lockdown relaxes it appears seeing family and friends has to be done in new ways, thinking of social distancing.

In these challenging times, reports say we have turned to chocolate, in July 2020 Retail Gazette reported one chocolatier seeing their sales online increase by 200%. We might have changed how we buy it, with online sales increasing but we have reached for our old favourite, chocolate.

My name is Anne Goodridge, and I am a life coach, a social worker, and a lover of life. I like to write, coach and to eat chocolate. Today, I get to do all three by sharing this with you, thank you.

What better way for me to share my thoughts about self-care than to eat a box of chocolates with you. We will discuss how each of those delicious chocolates can prompt you to consider how well you are looking after yourself.

The chocolate box is our smorgasbord of things to help us look after ourselves inside and out. I'll throw a few suggestions in, and there's room to make a few notes. Sometimes as we read or eat chocolate an idea forms and if we do not write it down there and then it's gone, melted away.

At the end of the book, there is a chance for you to make your selection of choc-o-care chocolates and plan to take care of yourself at the same time.

Look at all the choices we have when we are buying a box of chocolates. There are so many of them that there are shelves and aisles packed full of them in supermarkets. Not to mention the specialist chocolate shops!

Which chocolate we choose depends on a variety of factors.

How much money we have, who is it for and is it for a special occasion? What we know about the person's taste in chocolate, or is it for ourselves to eat straight away or enjoy later with family or friends?

When we have a box of chocolates, or one is offered for us to choose from one, the choice we make depends on what we like, what is left in the box, and if you're like me how much we are willing to be the one to have the last nutty one avoiding the strawberry cream! It's all a matter of taste. For example, I can hardly believe it, but some people's favourite is strawberry cream! Mine has to be a nutty one.

It is the same as looking after yourself, self-care.

There are numerous ways to look after ourselves; no one method fits all. Our choice depends on how we feel, what time we have, what outcome we want, what we can afford, and numerous other variables.

Just as I'm offering you chocolate from this box, I am offering you several different ways to look after yourself or put it another way, various self-care activities.

It is up to you to make a choice and then take action. No matter how many self-help books we read or how many YouTube videos we watch, you do not gain from your efforts unless you commit to taking action and then follow through with it. You can end up feeling worse as you are annoyed with yourself or disappointed with yourself for not taking action.

Like so many people I had collected self-help books, some I have read, and others remain on the shelf unread.

Over the years I gained a good understanding of self-care. I did try to have some exercise each week, and I learned a lot about the foods I should eat and those I should stop eating. I attended meditation courses, yoga classes and qualified as a reiki practitioner.

But a couple of years ago as things became more stressful in my life, I forgot to keep up my self-care practices.

Like so many of us, I tried to keep all my plates spinning, forgetting that the spinner needs to look after themselves. So I believe my body and mind said you are not listening, so they made me stop.

Physically I was depleted so ended up having surgery for something that various antibiotics would not heal. Mentally and emotionally, I was exhausted and needed to take time out. My body was yelling at me to stop.

I had all of this expertise, and while coaching others, I have published articles about self-care and written blog posts. But I still needed this wake-up call.

With the help of family friends, talking, and re-establishing my own self-care practice, I was able to replenish myself.

But, guess what, I guarantee you that during this time I did not have boxes and boxes of chocolate waiting for me to eat them, they were long gone, eaten without thinking about it!

In writing this book, I hope to remind you of the importance of self-care by taking the time it takes to eat a chocolate to think about it. I hope it will help you to choose to practice self-care as easy as selecting a chocolate.

Let's get started –

PICK AND MIX

Anyone, my age will remember the delights of the pick and mix counter at Woolworths. When Woolworths went out of business, it was the 'pick and mix' sweet experience that many people spoke about and still missed.

Like pick and mix, we all have our favourites in a chocolate box. How many times is the same chocolate left to the end because no one really likes it? It does not matter whether you prefer dark, milk, or white chocolate. Nutty, toffee, or soft centres, there is usually one we always look for first. All the chocolates will eventually get eaten.

Looking after ourselves is the same, self-care is all about our wellbeing. Books and experts might break it down to physical, mental, emotional, and spiritual needs. We all need to focus on the needs that come up in each of these areas at some time or other.

We might not always sit down and think, I'm going to focus my emotional wellbeing, but we know when we are out of sorts, feeling sad or lonely or full of joy and happiness, and there is something we can do to help.

Just as we know when we feel unfit, walking uphill has become a challenge, chasing the kids around is no longer the fun it was, as we puff and pant. We know then we should do something about our physical fitness. How we are feeling is a good indicator as to the state of our mental and emotional wellbeing.

Self-care is trending at the moment; you need to look at your newsfeed, open a magazine, or watch the TV. It's important to remember, as the following pages will show you it's not just about having a massage or watching a movie. It's about checking in on ourselves and asking 'how am I doing' and then taking action, taking small steps towards feeling better and improving wellbeing.

Treat this book as a pick and mix counter where you can fill your own box, not with chocolates but with lots of self-care activities.

It is worth pointing out now that the most effective and needed activity may not be your first choice. After all, if you enjoy physical exercise, you will potentially migrate towards reading one of the chocolates with a P in the heading. This is much like when choosing chocolate when we tend to choose our favourite first. I reach first for a nutty chocolate and ignore the others. Remember at this pick and mix counter to give other flavours a chance.

Self-care is sometimes thought of as being a bit wishy-washy, something for other people, but not me.

Today in all areas of life, we see and hear about the importance of looking after ourselves, from professional sports teams and players, the Armed Forces and the National Health Service, celebrities, workplaces, and home. The World Health Organisation recognises its importance, define it as

"the ability of individuals, families and communities to promote health, prevent disease, maintain health, and to cope with illness and disability with or without the support of a healthcare provider".

Over the years, I have often said to carers how important it is to look after themselves to be able to care and continue caring for their loved ones.

This is self-care, it is looking after our own self.

It is about the choices and actions we take to look after ourselves. Sometimes it is easier to see the value when we do it for someone else. An often-cited example is when we are on an airplane and the safety demonstration. The instruction is if we are travelling with children we should put our own oxygen mask on first before our children's. It can seem counter-intuitive, we want to help our child first, but we can understand that we can look after our children better if we can breathe.

Taking responsibility for ourselves is difficult; self-care can feel challenging. It can appear to go against all we have learnt and the things we say to ourselves such as;

"What are you doing that for, there are so many other things to be done."

"I should be looking after the children."

"I can't afford the time or money, and we need it for..."

"I'm not selfish, and it's selfish".

I believe that it is essential to find just a few minutes a day, to make a deliberate choice and take action to enhance our wellbeing. As a result, you will be happier, healthier. Much more able to do all the other pressing things on your 'to-do list', and they are more manageable.

I believe we have to start looking more holistically to look after ourselves & to maintain our wellbeing. By doing this, we become stronger and more able to live the life we want while managing the challenges that will inevitably come our way. It requires us to commit to and take consistent action.

Self-care does not have to mean adding lots more things to do in your already busy hectic day. As you eat through the chocolate box with me, I hope you'll find that sometimes it is about making small changes.

It might mean you decide to make a more significant change that has consequences for other things in your life, so that's going to involve thinking through the 'how's' and 'when's' and sometimes 'who' with. But do not be put off.

With all things start with small steps and with a sprinkle of fairy dust, made up of consistency, persistence, and that all-important patience. You will notice that you feel more energised, and happier and, on a really good day, ready to conquer your next challenge.

This book does not replace going to see the GP. If you have any underlying medical problems or are concerned about your health, go and seek medical advice. That in its self is self-care, you are looking after yourself.

While we are busy with our lives, this book aims to help you make time to look after yourself. To be most effective, you will need to be willing to take action, sample the techniques, and form a daily habit of self-care. I know I am repeating myself by saying this, but if you are like I used to be, I could quickly eat a chocolate a day if not two, but keeping a commitment to self-caring was another matter.

What's your favourite chocolate?

Take your pick – you can read from front to back, or you can select a chocolate at random or go for your favourite one.

All I would ask is that you do at some point look at the ones that are your least favourite as it may just be what you need and you could miss out.

Trying something new can help us feel well and stops us from getting into a rut. You might surprise yourself and find you like it.

At the end of this book, you will be ready to fill your own chocolate box full of your favourite ways of looking after yourself.

So as you read, be present and curious and commit to taking action.

Do You Know....

Switzerland consumes the most chocolate per person annually at a whopping 19.4pounds per capita. The UK is 16.8 pounds...and that means 1 in 6 people eat chocolate daily.

Worldatlas 27.09.2018

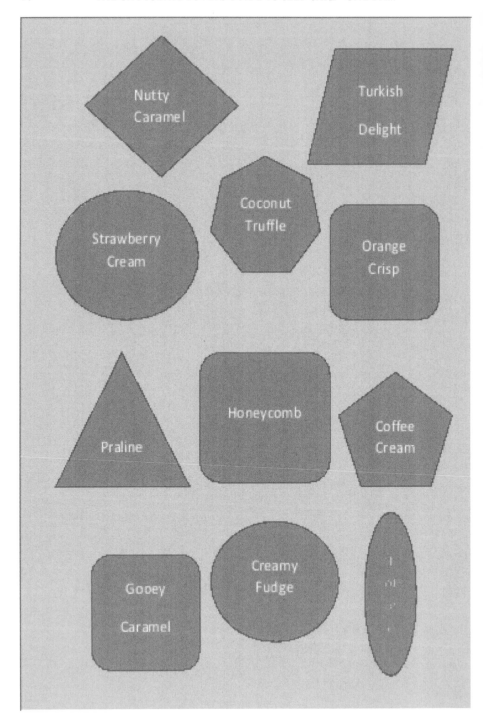

DO YOU KNOW....

Chocolate dates back to at least 450BC.

SELECTION TIME

I hope you are sat comfortably, maybe with a box of chocolates by your side.

When you look at the chocolates in this book, you will see I have placed them in a category that forms the Circle of Care – or in this book, the Choc-o-Care.

PHYSICAL (P), MENTAL (M), EMOTIONAL (E), AND SPIRITUAL (S).

PHYSICAL refers to your physical health, how fit you are, how your body is feeling. Do you have any illnesses or injuries and how they are affecting you? Is your physical health impacting on your self-care?

MENTAL refers to your mental health, your thoughts, and their impact on you. If you have any mental health issues, how are they impacting on you and your self-care?

EMOTIONAL is concerned with your feelings, how they may be impacting your physical health.

SPIRITUAL is concerned with your sense of purpose, and for some, it is also about faith. It is an essential element in the choc o care. It impacts on how we show up, how we care for others, and ourselves.

In the Choc o Care box there is no right or wrong section for a chocolate to be placed in, as you can see the circle of choc-o-care has no sharp delineations.

They flow into one another.

I have made my personal choices when putting chocolate in a particular section of choc o care, but you may change the position when you make up your box of choc o care.

After each chocolate there is space for you to make notes, doodle mind map and draw. If you do this as you are reading it may help you at the end, when you are filling your own choc o care book.

Just Before We Unwrap The Box Of Chocolates, Begin With A Quick Check-In With Yourself:

Do you take the time to look after yourself? Yes or No

Is self-care a part of your daily routine? Yes or No

Is your self-care routine balanced Yes or No

Do you take care of all the areas of the circle of choc o care? Yes or No

Do you set a time for daily self-care activities? Yes or No

Is that a resounding "yes", a "sometimes" an occasional or "I know I should but....." or a "no".

Some of us struggle to get from the *knowing and the thinking about* to the *doing*, from the reading or listening to taking action. But let's be honest unless you have an underlying health problem most of us do not have a problem eating chocolate, I hope that by the end of this book you will feel the same way about self-care.

Eat a Square of Chocolate –

There is some suggestion that a couple of squares of dark 85% chocolate a day helps lift your mood, so that's a WIN-WIN! But remember that chocolate does have fats and sugars in it, so moderation is required. To date, the NHS does not think there is enough evidence to recommend chocolate, even dark chocolate for health benefits.

There are times when we're so busy and stressed that we forget to check in with ourselves about how we are feeling.

Are you feeling your life is getting busier with so many demands on your time, feeling you have so many responsibilities, feeling guilty for not having time for the family or even the pets? Have you stopped doing the things you enjoy because of lack of time?

STOP....

Take time to have a square of chocolate and check-in with yourself.

How are YOU? Can you describe your mood?

Do a body scan? Can you feel any tension anywhere?

How well are YOU taking care of YOURSELF?

What's holding you back?

Make a note of your answers below.

_____
_____
_____
_____
_____
_____
_____
_____
_____
_____
_____
_____
_____
_____
_____
_____
_____

Use this space to be creative; doodle, Mind Map or Draw your thoughts and ideas.

As you read through the following pages, and maybe eat a chocolate or two, you will be able to take the time to consider your answers and then decide what will be in your choc-o-box of care.

The next section is about the chocolates you are likely to find in a box of chocolates.

DO YOU KNOW....

Chocolate originates from Mesoamerica.

NUTTY CARAMEL (P)

This chocolate can be tricky; it is chewy and can be challenging to eat. The combination of nuts, caramel, and chocolate swirl around your mouth as you eat.

It is a complex chocolate, with layers of flavours and textures. It can be tricky to eat, feeling like it takes up valuable time, sticking to your teeth.

Like the nutty caramel, exercise is complex. Exercise can be strenuous but ultimately leaves us feeling good. Exercise reduces anxiety and stress—releases feel-good serotonin.

We all know exercise is good for us. We can feel bombarded with this advice. We are reading about it on our screens, in newspapers and magazines. We hear lots of different people, including teachers, doctors, sports stars, politicians, TV personalities, all extolling benefits of exercise. We can see it, hear it and read it— all telling us the health benefits of getting fit. Our very own fit friends make suggestions to us or ask us to join them on a hike or cycle ride. Take a look on YouTube. There are numerous different classes we can participate in from the comfort of our living rooms.

I suspect that physical exercise is the area of self-care that we all know about and yet, for many, it's hard to practice. Many of us would instead choose a different choc o care than seriously consider making exercise a habit. That would mean we are committed to the daily activity of some kind that raises the heart level.

Then there are those of us who may have an intention, but never quite work towards fulfilling it. We know it's good for us, but something stops us.

We can give a multitude of reasons for that. Do any of these sound familiar?

"I'm too tired", "I don't like exercise", "I have no time", "I need to look after the children", "I can't afford a gym membership", "I'm too stressed" or "I don't have the equipment", "I've joined a gym before and not gone". "I'm injured", "I've never been good at sports", "and I hated PE at school".

I know that I can identify with some of these reasons. But perhaps it is time, to be honest with yourself, are they valid reasons or are they excuses?

I used to think "I don't have the time" or "I'm too stressed" and "I've got too much to do" fairly often, they would be reasons not to exercise or excuses.

Even knowing I love swimming, I still would not go!

Time to MAKE A DECISION

Key Questions to ask yourself

Do you know your WHY? Your reason for doing the exercise.

When it's cold and dark outside the WHY needs to be greater than the pulling power of the warmth of staying indoors.

Take a moment to write down your WHY, then commit to when and how often. Writing this down helps. It is also something to look at when you are wavering.

•   Make you're WHY something that excites and motivates YOU.

then ask

•   What might stop you from exercising?

What do you need to do to overcome these obstacles?

What kind of exercise have you enjoyed in the past?

The answers can be a clue to what you might find the best way to get started. The keyword here is ENJOY.

What amount of time are you willing to commit to exercise each week?

Make a note of your WHY

_____
_____
_____
_____
_____
_____

This keyword here is COMMIT. If you think I only have an hour to spare a week, it is no good saying you'll go to the local pool for a swim when travelling there and getting ready and takes you most of the hour you have earmarked. You will be put off from even setting off.

Is it more realistic to think of doing a workout each day following one of the many online exercise gurus? Or going for a walk in the hour you have found, just step out of your front door.

Are you still chewing the tasty Nutty Caramel? If so, this might be the time to mention your present health state.

Do you have a health problem that you need to consider before starting a new exercise? If so, seek advice from your Doctor.

Do you need to be with someone to keep committed and be accountable, an exercise/moving buddy? Who do you know that will exercise/moving with you? Do you need to find a personal trainer?

Some people thrive on having accountability, telling someone what they are doing or exercising with someone. For others, this time spent exercising is 'me' time, and they prefer to be on their own.

Just remember if you are going out alone, take safety precautions. Tell someone where you are going, your planned route, and take a charged mobile with you to summon help if ever required.

So still chewing on the nutty caramel, there is something else to consider when committing to exercise.

Choose what's right for you and then look for appropriate advice. This might include checking with your Doctor.

Then get set, you are ready to go.

Check out apps such as the NHS couch to 5k app to the numerous specialist clubs such as swimming clubs, football, squash, or Park runs.

Also if it's practical advice taking lessons to learn or relearn a sport can pay off in the long run, improving your skill and helping to prevent injury. If golf is your game, local golf clubs often have a golf pro attached to them who will give you a lesson to help improve your swing. Some personal trainers specialise in different approaches, group activities, and one to one coaching and training.

I like to go swimming twice a week. Afterwards, I feel brighter and alive. But there are times when I just don't go. Usually, it starts with some change in my weekly schedule that means I need to find another time to go to the pool, sometimes I've just got myself feeling too busy to go. I stress the word 'feeling' because I know that I can make time to go and feel better for swimming a few laps. To get back into a routine, I check in with myself, how am I feeling? What is happening around me?

Then look at my WHY before committing myself – what day and time I will go next week.

If organised exercise is not your thing, then incorporate more movement into your everyday life. Exercise does not have to cost you money, just opening the door and step outside, taking a walking will improve your health.

Parking the car when shopping – take the furthest spot in the car park from the exit, increase your steps, and increase the distance you are carrying your bags.

Public transport – can you get on and off a stop earlier or later.

Meeting a friend – meet and walk to the café, rather than meeting at the café for a coffee.

Put the TV remote on the other side of the room.

Walk around when you are talking on the phone.

How can you increase your movement during the day?

Remember if you are injured or have not exercised for a long time, chat with your Doctor before starting.

Make a note of your thoughts

_____
_____
_____
_____
_____
_____
_____
_____
_____
_____
_____
_____
_____
_____
_____

Use this space to be creative; Doodle, Mind Map or Draw your thoughts and ideas.

DO YOU KNOW…..

It is not known who first invented the Easter egg. They first appeared in France and Germany in the 19th Century. Cadburys records show that John Cadbury first made a "French Eating Chocolate Egg" in 1842 but did not produce Easter Eggs until 1875.

HONEYCOMBED
BATON (P, M, E, S)

Honeycomb is sweet, can be crispy and chewy at the same time. Nature's gold wrapped in chocolate. I am conjuring up pictures of bees in their hives working hard to produce honey. Bees pollinate flowers, plants and are one of the signs of a healthy environment.

"bees are the batteries of orchards, gardens, guard them."

Carol Ann Duffy, The Bees

On their website, Friends of the Earth state that "Bees are a great indicator of a healthy environment."

For centuries honey has been food and medicine. Today we recognise its magical properties, as well as using it as a natural sweetener. Honey is a source of natural antioxidents and has many health benefits. For example, the World Health Organisation recommends honey as a cough remedy.

While I cannot claim that the honeycomb in the chocolate has many health benefits, it reminds us of the great outdoors and that being outdoors is good.

We spend so much time in front screens, whether for work, education, or entertainment. We read about detoxing from technology, switching off our devices, and spending the time together or having 'me time'. Parents worrying about the amount of screen time their children are having.

During the first coronavirus lockdown period in the UK, people were permitted to take 1 hour's exercise outdoors a day. The government recognised the importance of spending time outdoors to a healthy population.

Taking the time to stroll outdoors for as much time as you can manage is a form of self-care. Like honey, it has multiple benefits, that's why I have highlighted all four areas of the circle of choc-o-care, Physical, Emotional, Mental and Spiritual.

By being outdoors, we can increase our Vitamin D intake, at least when the sun is shining.

Being outdoors in a green space can help to reduce stress. A study by Mathew White et al. of the University of Exeter published in Nature.com 13 June 2019 found that people were more likely to report good health and psychological wellbeing by spending two hours a week outdoors in green spaces.

So two hours, that's 120min over a week can be broken down to just 18 minutes a day, or two longer sessions of an hour. Two hours a week is a doable amount of time for most of us, think how good you could feel if you did spend two hours a week in green spaces. Yes, it includes dog walking, taking the children out for a walk, or playing a game outdoors. If you live in an urban setting, explore the green spaces close by you, whether that's a square, or a park or playing fields.

Have you considered walking a healthy form of exercise, a time to be mindful, a time to think, or a time for an adventure? If you listen to Ramblings on BBC Radio 4, you will hear Claire Balding taking a walk in the countryside with people who know the particular walk and want to share it. Some common themes come up, the love of the outdoors, the positive impact being outdoors had on their wellbeing, and many other things.

I am biased as I love walking, in 2016 I wrote an article in Hen-picked, an online magazine, entitled 'Walking therapy: the power of the outdoors' where I talk further about walking and its impact on my mood.

Have you ever thought about how you actually walk? How we

walk can reflect how we are feeling. How are you standing, are you standing tall, open and with a smile lighting your face, or are you bent over and just looking at the ground? It can give others as well as ourselves an insight into how we are feeling. When I'm feeling well, and on good form, my walk is that much lighter, I am definitely taller, which is an excellent thing for someone who is only 5ft 4 inches. I notice more things around me more.

Walking is a perfect form of exercise to become aware of how you feel and the different experience of seeing things in more detail than our view from the car.

Use ALL your senses -

What can you see around you?

Look all around you, turning your head from side to side, looking up and down.

What colours do you see? What is around you? How is the light changing the shapes and the shadows? Are the clouds racing across the sky? Depending on the time of day, is the sun shining, or are there stars in the sky?

If you want to stop to take a closer look at something that has caught your attention, just stop.

What can you hear?

Listen there are the unmistakable initial sounds, but others make up the familiar soundscape if you listen carefully.

What can you taste?

Is it sweet, sour, salty, bitter, sweet, or metallic? Can you place where you are by tasting it, are there different flavours? Did you know we tend to taste sweet things at the front of our mouths and bitter towards the back?

What can you feel?

As you walk, be aware of the sensation of the air on your face, is it cold, warm, clammy, or hot?

What is your foot touching? Even in shoes, we can tell the difference between grass and pavement, track and trail.

All the senses work together to give an overall picture of the scene. But by focusing on just one of the senses, we can isolate the sensation.

Try it and notice how walking becomes that much more enjoyable.

Another beneficial outdoor activity is gardening. Monty Don is quoted in House Beautiful 18th May 2020 as saying that gardening "nourishes the soul." Gardening is a self-care activity. Weeding and digging and mowing and cutting hedges all help you to become stronger and flexible. Tending to plants is also good for our mental and emotional life.

Nurturing growth in the garden and reaping its benefits with fresh fruit and vegetables is for some a spiritual experience. Gardening focuses our mind on the task at hand. Being mindful and present can help to reduce our everyday worries and improve our wellbeing.

So can you take 2 hours a week and get outdoors into a green space. Commit today.

What activity are you going to choose, gardening, fishing, golf, swimming, hiking, Frisbee, dog walking, painting, butterfly counting, the list is endless.

Make a note of your thoughts and ideas.

_____
_____
_____
_____

Use this space to be creative; Doodle, Mind Map or Draw your thoughts and ideas.

DO YOU KNOW….

In times gone by, chocolate was once used as a form of currency. The cacao bean was valued by the Mayan and Aztec and used as a form of money.

CREAM FUDGE (P, E)

Chocolate encasing a surprisingly silky, rich, creamy and buttery fudge that melts in your mouth just like treating yourself to a pamper—something to indulge in on occasions.

"Sometimes, all we need is a little pampering to help us feel better..." Charles M. Schulz, Peanuts Guide to Life: Wit and Wisdom from the World's Best-Loved Cartoon Characters

Yes, self-care or looking after yourself can mean making time to treat yourself to a pampering session. There are times when we need to make space to pamper ourselves.

The Collins Dictionary definition of .to pamper 'is to treat with affectionate and usually excessive indulgence; coddle; spoil.'

Self-care means different things to different people. But whatever you choose, it takes time. Something that we do not feel we have enough of.

When we are busy trying to look after our families, young and old, and those in between, manage our home, working or seeking work, education, and juggling the demands on our time can mean that the easiest one to squeeze out of contention is you. We will say things like

"I haven't got time."

"I'll wait till....,"

"Oh, it's not important."

"I can do that later."

These are signs of a helper or a pleaser, wanting to help everyone, to please everyone. At the extreme, this can lead to exhaustion and burnout. You are feeling exhausted, physically and emotionally, but still having to juggle a million things.

In coaching sessions, people have said things such as, "I want everyone to be happy and if not happy, ok" and "finding 'my time' is difficult".

One simple way of creating 'my time ' is to wake up earlier than you presently do. Setting the alarm 5 minutes is a good start, then gradually increase the time by 5 mins, before long you are getting up 30 miniutes earlier. This becomes 'my time', no matter what else was going on.

We can become so accustomed to not cherishing 'my time'. Saying "Yes" without thinking. We need to   stop the automatic response and step back before responding. Asking 'have I got the time', 'do I want to do this', 'what impact will this have on all the other things I am doing'. Then the big one ' do I want to say YES or NO'. If your answer is No, what is stopping me saying NO. When we have yet another demand, it takes a conscious effort to take the steps to change our routine way of responding.

When setting out our intentions, making the time, let those around us know, this is 'my time', we have to be deliberate about it. It only takes a few times before others accept that this is your time and not disturb you. Maybe the children are going out with their friends, and you can arrange for younger children to be looked after by family or friends and you reciprocate the arrangement. The adults you share your home with need to know this is your time and firmly told no disturbances. Sometimes it's a matter of finding a time that suits everyone.

In finding this time, do not be put off or distracted from your end goal. Whatever it is, whether its a relaxing home spa experience or time to nourish your hands and feet with lotion and a manicure and pedicure. Remember this is your time for refuelling, to relax, and refresh.

By doing this, you show others that you value yourself and more importantly, you show yourself that you are important. It will also be good for your body to unwind. If you are thinking of creating a home spa experience, you will feed your soul and body.

It is time to unplug and relax. For some, the idea of soaking in a bath is an absolute no-no, but taking a long shower to unwind from the day could be heaven. We can all enjoy a home spa, using our favourite lotions.

The key to this is to gift yourself the time and space to enjoy and not to feel guilty about it. Go on book an appointment with yourself, put it on the calendar or in your diary. Choose a room for your pamper session; make sure it's warm enough.

Do you want music? Make up a playlist. Are you going to read, have the magazine or book close at hand? You do not want to be hunting around for them when you are relaxing.

Tell everyone in the house, you are not to be disturbed. Do not feel guilty about this. YOU need this time.

Have the things around you that will help you feel pampered these might be aromatherapy oils, hand cream, nail varnish. Or it could be the travel section of the paper and a lovely croissant. It's your choice.

Remember that there are times when we need to think of pamper on a small scale. We can all take 10 minutes a day to use hand cream to moisturise our hands. Now that we are washing our hands more and using hand sanitizer it is even more important to do this. But we can just rush it thinking of other things, or we can take our time. Focusing on each part our hand, each finger and thumb, first the left and then the right. Being aware of our breathing as we do this, slowing our breath and enjoying the fragrance of the cream as well as the sensation of stroking our hands.

If it is not your hands, then maybe you can find 10 minutes to look after your feet. They carry you where ever you want to go, so giving them some valuable papmering time is going to be beneficial. As with your hands, use a lotion that is going to soak in as you massage each foot. Making sure that you have massage each toe individually. Your feet will thank you, I promise.

Go ahead, make your preparations and enjoy.

Make a note of the things that will make you feel pampered.

Use this space to be creative; Doodle, Mind Map or Draw your thoughts and ideas.

DO YOU KNOW....

Chocolate Houses appeared in London from 1657 frequented by royalty, and the wealthy to drink chocolate and perhaps plan some intrigue.

TURKISH DELIGHT (E)

This taste of the Orient is a delicious jelly scented with exotic flavour and perfume with rose water coated in chocolate. It evokes magical dreams, thoughts of eastern mystery, or memories of a holiday.

"Once a year, go somewhere you have never been before." Dalai Lama

Now is the time to talk with your partner, 'best friend' or family member. Someone you have shared an adventure, experience or holiday with or someone you are planning to share an experience, adventure, or holiday.

Book an evening meal at your favourite restaurant, or have your favourite take away.

or

Cook a meal that reminds you of the holiday. Reminisce about the fun times you had on holiday. Start planning your next one.

Be sure to have some no-go conversation agreements – such as talk about work, home renovations, even the kids, unless it's to laugh, remembering their look when they came face to face with a camel for the first time.

You get the picture, dream, and escape and have fun together.

 Or

Sit down and look at your photos, don't rush, look closely, and remember the scene, the noises, taste, and how things felt.

Now you're in the mood for the exotic, have you a bucket list? The places you would like to travel too or experiences you would like to have? How many have you ticked off?

I dream and think about where in the world I would like to visit. The internet allows me to roam around the world faster than Phileas Fogg. I love maps, seeing where I've been and looking at places I'd like to go too.

There are numerous travel programmes on the TV full of ideas of places to see and different expereinces that are available. It does not matter whether you want a hot or cold climate, a beach holiday, city break or mountian walking and more, there is something for every one.

But travel does not always need to be to distant parts. There are lots of beautiful parts of the this country.   Sometimes it is the places on our own doorsteps that we forget about.

I love the outdoors and enjoy camping. I know not everyone will find the connection between eating a turkish delight and camping that easy to make! But for me it is, yes I have had my fair share of wet and windy camping holidays. But I have also memories of waking up in the mornining seeing the sun rise, loving the clean freshness of the air, and the colours in the tent. The simplicity of life when camping. I love it as much as I love turkish delights.

You might be reminded of a day trip to the seaside, or to the courtyside or a trip to London to see the sights or go to the theatre.

Travel is as big or as small, as far or as close as you want it to be. It is is as much to do with our mindset as it is mileage. If we set off with a curious and inquisitive mind, open to new expereinces then we will be open to adventure anywhere we go.

 If you have not made a list of places to go to, things you want to see and experience, think about it now, start to create one now.

But remember to take your time over it, look up places, watch films, listen to music, and read about them.

Think about the many different ways you could take to travel there. Are you going overland, by boat or air?

I once walked 500 miles carrying all the things I needed on my back. This was walking the Camino De Santiago, a journey I had thought about many times over many decades. I'd watched films and read many books before it was actually possable. This trip brought all my senses alive, I met people from all over the world, lived simply, with a daily routine of get up, eat, walk, eat, sleep, and repeat day after day for 500 miles.

I saw the most amazing sites, I can still smell the eucalyptus forest. I can still taste the crisp cold water from the water fountains along the way. Taking the time to travel slowly was a pleasure, one that I can relive easily. One that still excites me.

What holiday do you remember?

Are you planning one now?

Ask yourself why you are drawn to these particular places? Is it your mood now, the person you pecieve yourself to be?

As you eat your turkish delight let your mind roam free...you just might surprise yourself.

Make a note of your bucket list.

_____
_____
_____
_____
_____
_____
_____

Use this space to be creative; Doodle, Mind Map or Draw your thoughts and ideas.

DO YOU KNOW....

At the time of the French Revolution, hot chocolate was thought to be an aphrodisiac.

PRALINE (M S)

There are many descriptions of praline. Is it French or Belgium, does it have nuts added or is it soft-centred? That's going to depend on the particular chocolate you are eating. It is a paste of nuts, sugar and vanilla Take a moment to experience an explosion of sensations on your tongue as you bite into this particular chocolate, is it soft-centred or hard?

Like a praline, we cannot always tell what will make us laugh. Our humour varies from one person to another, and from one time to another.

"You need to laugh" Maya Angelou.

Laughter is good for us. Have you ever listened to someone laughing, is it infectious?

I can recall laughing with friends and family, when I try to remember why we laughed, I cannot put my finger on what was so funny. When I was 18, I went out for a meal with my parents, and during the conversation, we started to laugh, and to this day if any one of us mentions this particular meal we smile and laugh together. Was there a joke that set it off? No, it was just a story about a man travelling from Yorkshire to the Isle of Wight for the day. Now on paper that's not fun, but trust me, it's guaranteed to make my family laugh.

We are laughing at ourselves, remembering how we laughed, remembering the feeling of being together, and enjoying one another's company.

Then, there are the times I laughed so much with friends we were crying and laughing we could not stop, again just a name can set us off, and it can be years on from the event.

We do not have to be with other people to laugh. Have you ever burst out laughing while you are reading or watching a comedy.

Laughter makes us feel good; it's contagious, and it is joyful. Laughter relaxes us, helps to release stress and releases endorphines. They are the hormones that relieve pain and improve our well being.

On You tube there are clips of people laughing under the heading contagious laughter. Have you been on a train or bus when one person starts to laugh. It is guarenteed that others will begin to smile and laugh without knowing what is funny.

Children are not self-conscious about laughing. Watch a group of children playing, and you will hear laughter. As we grow older, we become more aware of situations and circumstances that are inappropriate to laugh. While it's true we should always be mindful of laughing at someone, it is hurtful and therefore harmful to them, and us, but laughing with someone can be very beneficial.

No matter who we are, heads of state, royalty, bosses, you and me, everyone enjoys laughing.

There are times when laughter can help to build a bridge between people. When the nitty-gritty of business is set aside over lunch and by relaxing, people share a joke or two. Laughter can help us to relax, and when business commences again more gets done.

When did you last have a really good laugh? Do you ever laugh when you are on your own? Maybe when you read a book, something sets you off, or thought has popped into your head, and you cannot stop yourself laughing.

Make a go-to list of things that are guaranteed to make you laugh. It could include YouTube clips, TV programmes, or films that give you that feel-good feeling. You know the one, that feeling that lifts you. These are just a few of my favourite funny things, Fleabag, anything by Victoria Wood, Not Going Out and Allen Carr. Our lists will be different because we all have our own individual sense of humour, but taking the time to think about what makes you laugh will give you a greater understanding of your own sense of humour. Share your list with others, tell others about that new comedy you have watched that had you roaring. They may have missed it.

Laughing can make you feel good; it relaxes your face muscles, reduces stress, and increases your oxygen levels. It is a full work out for your facial muscles.

Time to have a laughter work out. Earlier I mentioned how laughter is contagious, have you noticed how infectious laughter is.

Try a burst of forced laughter and see how long it is before you are actually laughing? Then notice how long it is before those around you laugh.

Where ever you are RIGHT NOW stand up and start to laugh, at first it will feel forced, but before long you will be laughing.

One of the best workshops I have ever been too was a laughter workshop. Standing with people I did not know following the instructions on laughing was a truly feel good expereince.

I recommend you check out where your local Yoga Laughter workshop is and book yourself a place. I can guarantee you will have a good time laughing. Perhaps a Comedy Club is more of your thing or a rerun of your favourite comedy.

Make a note of your go-to laughter places.

_____
_____
_____
_____
_____
_____

_____
_____
_____
_____
_____
_____
_____
_____
_____
_____
_____
_____

Use this space to be creative; Doodle, Mind Map or Draw your thoughts and ideas.

DO YOU KNOW....

White chocolate is not really chocolate! Yes, that's right, because it does not contain cocoa solids White Chocolate is not chocolate.

TOFFEE (M)

Crunch your way through this or try to make it last as long as possible. The chocolate hides a toffee centre that is silky but sticks to your teeth. These are ideal for eating when thinking.

"The nice thing about doing a crossword puzzle is, you know there is a solution." Stephen Sondheim

We are beginning to learn more about our brain's plasticity or neuroplasticity, how the brain adapts and changes. It does not matter what age we are by learning new things; our brains create new neuropathways and networks, which can help us manage change and adapt to new things around us.

But do not worry, this chocolate is about fun and enjoyment. No matter how much you enjoy your work, this is about play, switching off from work, giving your work brain a rest.

So put your thinking cap on, self-care is not just about a soak in a bath you know. During the lockdown, people have rediscovered their love of jigsaws and board games such as Monopoly, Scrabble and Cluedo, playing card games, and games such as chess.

I enjoy puzzling over the pieces of a jigsaw. On many a holiday with friends, we have had a communal jigsaw going throughout the stay. Often there has been a mad dash to finish it before the last day of the holiday.

I enjoy a quick crossword, but the cryptic crossword still mystifies me. Maybe if I'm ever cast-off to a desert island, I'll take a compilation of cryptic crosswords and a guide to learn how to crack the codes.

Time to try a new activity or one you have not done for a while

Puzzle over a crossword, Sudoku, or word search or any other brain teaser of your choice.

A jigsaw puzzle, something for all the household.

Try learning something new. It could be learning to play that musical instrument you've always wanted to play. Or learning a new language, perhaps one you can use on your next holiday.

Be James Bond; your mission 007 is to break a code. There are lots of puzzle books around.

If you have pen and paper handy try drawing a map of the streets where you live without looking them up. How well do you know your local area? How far away from your home can you still name the roads? Perhaps you know your daily routes but are not sure what is around them? What places of interest are there? Do you know any local history, add it to your masterpiece. Are there places that are special to you? Have you included your family and friends houses? You can make this map just for you or your household. You could encourage them to add their places of interest. But most importantly, have fun with it.

Read a book or article about a subject you know nothing about, something outside your usual read. Going outside your comfort zone, you might find something new you enjoy.

I am sure you can come up with your own suggestions, it may be something you do on your own or together with family or friends, but start chewing on your toffee and give this a go.

Make a note of the ideas you have had.

_____
_____
_____
_____
_____
_____

Use this space to be creative; Doodle, Mind Map or Draw your thoughts and ideas.

DO YOU KNOW....

You can travel the world, going to museums dedicated to chocolate. January 2021, Wikipedia has 62 museums listed and in every continent.

GOOEY CARAMEL. (S)

It is oozing a sticky sweet flavour. Is this one of your favourites? If so just take a moment to chew this mindfully and savour the flavours that flow around your mouth as the luscious, buttery-soft caramel escapes its chocolate encasement.

Small moments of mindfulness throughout the day can change how we feel. So what is mindfulness, there are many books, courses, classes, and YouTube films devoted to explaining mindfulness and showing or guiding people in a mindful practice.

In Mindfulness for Beginners Jon Kabat-Zinn describes mindfulness as "paying attention: on a sustained and particular way: on purpose, in the present moment, and non-judgmental".

It's shifting from doing to being, but as he says "through the application of attention and awareness".

As a lover of chocolate, I have no intention of giving up chocolate. Instead, I'm using it as a tool to help me move from doing to being and with that be more relaxed and manage my stress better.

Talking about chocolate and especially Gooey Caramel in the same sentence as mindfulness may seem as if I am trivialising things. But I am genuinely not.

When we are busy in our 'doing' mode, practising mindfulness is rushed away by the 'to do' list. Even if mindfulness has reached your 'to-do list' when you get to it, you might be wanting to add it on tomorrow's list. This happens because we tend to be living life at a fast pace, feeling we have not got time to do everything. Then anything to do with ourselves, our self-care gets put on hold.

We have coped with Coronavirus's effect this past year, and our lifestyles have changed. For many, the rushing around from place to place is replaced with a mental rushing. Worry and anxiety about today and the future, how to juggle child care, home schooling, teaching and work, caring for someone, are just a few things that whirl around our minds.

You may be surprised to read that in 2018 Microsoft research concluded that the average person's concentration time is now 8 seconds, which has reduced from 12 seconds in 2000.

So, suppose when you are eating a gooey caramel, you are reminded to take a moment to be aware of the taste and all its different flavours hitting different notes in your mouth, noticing the differing textures, and taking in the aroma. In that case, you will have been eating mindfully at that moment. Which depending on how gooey the caramel is will be longer than 8 seconds? That has to be good news.

There are many places you can look for more information on mindfulness, and there are classes in mindfulness run locally, there are books to read and films to watch, apps to download, and people you can talk to about mindfulness. I have a library of books and as well as downloaded apps.

But what I found I needed most was to be more consciously aware of making the time to practice mindfully. This lovely gooey caramel helps me to do just this.

Similar to starting exercise, we need to have WHY that is important to us to make the practice of mindfulness important enough to give our time and focus on it.

I am not an expert. For me, meditation is a part of mindfulness. It is also about being present and trying to slow down. To not worry about what has past or about what is to come. It is to remember to focus on my breathing, especially in a stressful situation.

Breathwork is a topic all on its own.

Breathing is something we do without thinking, awake and sleeping.

When I stop an think about breathing I instantly feel and hear the air coming in and going out as I breath. I become aware of how I am breathing.

I have learnt, that if I stop and focus on a few deep breaths I feel more relaxed. I am able to focus more clearly on whatever it is I'm dealing with. So I do recommend that at some point in the day you stop and take a few deep breaths.

It will be more helpful to do this when you are doing a small action you repeat during the day such as, puting the kettle on for a drink, rather than when you are eating a chocolate. I do not want anyone choking. But the action then becomes the trigger to remind you to focus on your breath.

If something happens and you feel yourself getting tense, negative thoughts are in your head, feeling overwhelmed or perhaps notice you are running round trying to keep everything going. Stop and focus on your breath.

Youtube has a number of videos demonstrating breathing exercises, including mindful breathing, Calm Breath Bubble and Dr Weil's. I have used Dr Weil's 4,7,8 technique, this is simply breathing in for 4 holding your breath for 7 and breathing out for 8.

Remember breath awareness

Make a note of your thoughts and ideas.

_____
_____
_____
_____
_____

Use this space to be creative; Doodle, Mind Map or Draw your thoughts and ideas.

DO YOU KNOW....

Princess Mary sent chocolate to the troops in WW1.

ORANGE CRISP (P)

Eating this chocolate, you taste the zingy flavour of the orange bursting in your mouth, sizzling on your tongue. There is a sharpness and a zest for life that oozes out when eating an orange crisp. Bright refreshing and cheering, dance around the kitchen turn the radio up.

Now is the time to be moving, really moving. It does not matter if you are alone, with your family or friends, it's time to move that body.

"And hand in hand, on the edge of the sand, they danced by the light of the moon, the moon, the moon, they danced by the light of the moon."

Edward Lear The Owl and the Pussycat.

Dancing to music is good for us, whether we are alone or with others, it gets the heartbeat racing, you cannot help but smile, and your soul sings. When did you last spontaneously start moving to the music?

Watch young children, apart from the fact they never seem to sit still, they jig about, no qualms about being self-conscious, or worrying about who is watching.

As adults, we have tended to forget the pleasure of dancing, or we have become self-conscious about how we might look. Worrying about others seeing us, worrying what they might think and worse still say.

The BBC's programme Strictly Come Dancing is loved by many, it has consistently high viewing figures. We love to watch, some of us secretly wish we could make those moves, offering the contestants advice from our armchairs and gasping with delight when an audacious move is successful. We watch as a complete beginner falls in love with dance. I enjoyed dancing as a child. I took Ballroom, Modern and Latin dance classes. I still like to have a go, but watching the professionals and contestants leaves me in awe of their talent, energy and rhythm. Most of all, their joy is contagious.

Dancing has multiple benefits and boosts our heart rate, it is a weight-bearing exercise, so it helps to strengthen our bones. It can also improve balance and flexibility, not to mention possibly helping with weight loss.

Like other physical exercises, it can lift our mood, giving us that feel-good feeling, it also has a positive impact on our self-confidence. Dancing to music means we have another double whammy of goodness.

Music has the power to lift our moods, help us cope with stress, not to mention see us through difficult times. I have some go to music if I want to lift my mood. I am sure you have too.

Latin, ballet, jazz , tap, folk, irish, ballroom, hip hop contempory and the list goes on. We can learn differnt styles of dance, going to classes or watching others. But the dancing we do for ourselves in our kitchen does not have to conform to any set style. We just need to let ourselves go.

Tune your radio into a music station and dance.

Get yourself a dance playlist together so you can dance at any time. Share your playlist with your friends, add to it regularly.

Dance is exercise, even if we dance along just to one song. The average record played on the radio is around 3 minutes long, so let's get jigging.

Feeling that 'Strictly' feeling, then there is nothing to stop you find out where you can learn the magical dance steps yourself. Yes, there are online lessons so you can start at home. But, there are many classes out there where you can learn alongside others. Dancing with others takes it to a whole new level. Once you have got over wondering if everyone else is looking at you and realised no, they too are concentrating on their steps, you can enjoy the shared energy.

The next time you eat an orange crisp, smile and tap your feet and move your hips.

Move your body, shake it out, and dance.

Make a note of what music gets you moving and create a playlist.

Use this space to be creative; Doodle, Mind Map or Draw your thoughts and ideas.

DO YOU KNOW……

Oompa-Loompas & scrumdiddlyumptious are made-up words from 'Charlie and the Chocolate Factory.' R.D-hal

STRAWBERRY CREAM (E, S)

Soft centre chocolate oozing the taste of summer. Chocolate encasing a bite of the sweet fruity taste of sunshine.

Strawberries are said to have many health benefits for us, rich in vitamin C and antioxidants.

They can be eaten just as they are. We can pick our own or buy them in punnets.

For me, strawberries and cream, go together like Wimbledon and tennis. If you are a tennis fan and are lucky enough to have tickets to the final then you are more than likely to be feeling thankful for the tickets and grateful for the possibility of strawberries and cream, or is that just me!

If you are interested in self-development, you will not be surprised to see I have included Gratitude in this box of Choco Care.

When I was growing up after Christmas and birthdays, my parents made sure I wrote thank-you letters to our relatives for the presents they had given us. I'm sure the aunt or uncle receiving one from me would a) have known that my parents had a hand in getting me to write the letter, b) be pleased to receive it and c) had a chuckle at my spelling. As a child, I think I meant the thank you, but I know I was eager to finish and get back to playing.

A daily practice of Gratitude is on a deeper level than my childhood thank you letters, you will be pleased to hear.

Daily Gratitude about appreciating what you have, not just the material things in your life but all things in life.

It involves taking the time to *feel* thankful.

There are days and times when it is easy to feel Gratitude when everything is going well. Maybe the sun is shining, or if you're a skier there is snow on the piste, or you have a memorable day as your child stands on their own for the first time, or at work, you have a success.

These are times when we smile knowingly and at the end of the day can easily recall the feelings these events have evoked in us, and we can feel Gratitude.

Sometimes we are faced with challenging times and to contemplate Gratitude seems absurd. Developing a routine of being grateful helps on these days. You will find something that you can appreciate, something you witnessed or heard, touched or tasted that you can add to your gratitude list.

It might be something small that you would usually overlook.

I have to say that there are times when it is more challenging to be grateful. But even in our darkest times, I have found something to appreciate.

I notice the small things that can make the difference, how the suns ray are catching a leaf or the smell in the air after the rain. Maybe it is the taste of morning coffee, or a comment passed my way or the touch by a friend or family member.

We can show appreciation for our loved ones, friends, and work colleagues. But what about the person we find difficult, or we disagree with? Perhaps then we are looking to appreciate what we have learned about ourselves from our encounters. Not always easy to do, but worth thinking about.

Does this seem a long way from the Strawberry Cream that has sent it rays of sunshine dancing in our mouths? Positive psychology research has shown both a physical and mental health benefit to our well being for those who follow a practice of Gratitude.

For us who are looking at different ways to make self-care a priority to improve our physical and mental health, then this is something we can practice daily.

Have a go, commit to practice Gratitude for at least a week and see how you are feeling and what you are noticing. You could write a daily gratitude list or keep a gratitude journal. If you like it continue after the week.

Another example is to remember when saying thank you to someone and tell them why, how they have made you feel, or what they have enabled you to do.

Use Gratitude as a part of being mindful. For example take three things that you are grateful for and one by one focus all your attention on that one thing, what it looks like, how it sounds, does it have a taste or smell. How does your Gratitude for it feel? Hold that feeling for a time. Then go to the next one.

or

Have a gratitude jar. Write a note or a gift tag and put it in a jar. Read them when you find it hard to practice Gratitude, maybe your mood has dropped, or you have a head full of negative talk.

The Strawberry Cream is a bundle of thankfulness wrapped in chocolate.

Make a note of your thoughts.

_____
_____
_____
_____
_____
_____

Use this space to be creative: Doodle, Mind Map or Draw your thoughts and ideas.

DO YOU KNOW....

In the 17th Century, people liked to be seen drinking hot chocolate in their best parlour while discussing the affairs of the day.

COFFEE CREAM (M, E)

A coffee cream has that mellow flavour of a good cup of coffee. It's smooth enough to mean we languish over it without rushing.

"Never underestimate the power of a good cup of coffee." Ursula Vernon author

We have become used to grabbing and going with a flat white, cappuccino, or the skinny dipping lactose-free latte.

Instead of grabbing and go whatever your cuppa, coffee or tea, grab one and speak to a friend. You might even have a regular coffee club where friends and family support one another. You can do this over zoom or skype, so it's not always necessary to go out.

Having a sense of connection enhances our wellbeing. If we feel connected, it helps us to combat that hollow feeling of loneliness.

So as you taste the coffee centre of this chocolate consider who your social support group is. It might be family, friends, colleagues, or acquaintances. Now think about when was the last time you spoke to them.

Consider each person, what role do they play in supporting you.

They could be a motivator, that person you can rely on to encourage you because they believe in you and know you can achieve your dreams. They are the ones that will stand for hours watching marathon runners go by waiting for you to cheer you on at the 18th mile, just because they know you will are likely to be be flagging and want to cheer you on. They are the one that remembers the anniversary or seemingly unknowingly reaches out to you when you are feeling like 'it's just too much' or the pesky voice of "I can't", or I'm not good enough has whispered in your ear and stopped you in your tracks.

Then there is your play pal. You know the one that's happy to take part in your antic's, the one who goes swimming at dawn with you, laughs over hot chocolate and a little toddy or decides you're both going to volunteer to take part in the local carnival. This person is going to lift you just by being with you. Who can chat away and the time flies by. Who is your play pal, when did you last spend time together?

Don't let life get in the way; we all need the people who bring the colour of fun and laughter in our lives.

Who else is in your corner, who dares to tell you when they think you are going off course, who can tell you are wrong in a way that you listen too? They are likely to be a person you trust, who is not afraid to say "What the heck are you doing". More importantly, it is someone we listen to, consider what they have said, and then make your decision to carry on or think again before we act.

Who is your role model? It might be a mentor, colleague or a friend or someone you follow on social media or who speaks out for a cause you think is cool. They seem to manage life, just like you are aiming to. Spend time learning more about them, if possible, spend some time with them, and speak to them about your goals and ideas.

When I was planning to walk the Camino de Santiago, I met with a friend's friend who had walked it twice. He gave me lots of useful tips and enjoyed sharing his experience with me. Since completing it, I have shared my experience with others, both individually and speaking, to groups allowing me to pass on my hints and tips.

Remember, people like to help, asking for advice can feel challenging, but people often appreciate being asked. After all, spending the time it takes to have a coffee and give you a few hints and tips allows them to be the giver and share their experiences and expertise. You never know what gems might come your way.

Your support group all works together to support you and help you live your desired life.   But to do this, you need to stay in contact.

Do you know what role you play in their lives? Think about it, have a chat about it, celebrate it.

Our social support groups are best when cherished, like a plant, nurtured watered, feed, and given daylight they flourish. Friendships are like a coffee cream chocolate, rich, bittersweet, or smooth; all are to be enjoyed.

List of the people in your support group. Can you identify the roles people play?

_____
_____
_____
_____
_____
_____

Make time for a coffee and a chat, in person, on the telephone or via Zoom, Skype, or your choice of social media.

Make a note of your thoughts.

_____
_____
_____
_____
_____
_____
_____
_____

Use this space to be creative Doodle, Mind Map or Draw your thoughts and ideas.

DO YOU KNOW....

If you are lucky enough to own 'Le Chocolate Box' you own the most expensive box of chocolates in the world, at $1.5 million.

COCONUT CHOCOLATE TRUFFLE (P,M,E)

Coconut truffles are both soft and hard at the centre. The desiccated coconut rolled around the chocolate centre adds a taste of paradise, a luxurious tropical flavour.

Have you ever held a coconut in your hand, its shell is hard and rough to the touch? But inside it hides a delicious surprise of white meat and water. The coconut plays with your senses.

I have had the good fortune and delight of eating a coconut straight from the tree. I watched a person cut it down, slicing the top off to reveal the coconut's jewels. Drinking the coconut water, oh my how delicious was that.

So tasting coconut for me evokes happy thoughts.

What does the coconut remind you of? It might be all the fun of the fair for some people, for others, it might be more of a sigh remembering how difficult it can be to crack open a coconut!

Any book that talks about chocolate cannot be seen as a guide to healthy eating. But the beautiful coconut has a multitude of uses.

It can be eaten straight from the shell, in cooking and baking. We can drink coconut water or make a smoothie or use coconut milk. It can be a reminder to pause and think about our diet for a moment.

This chocolate, the coconut truffle, is a reminder to eating healthy and keeping hydrated to stay well.

When you take a bite of this chocolate, pause and think about the qualities of the coconut and ask yourself the following questions;

How healthy is my diet this week?

Is it balanced, with five a day of fruit and veg?

How much have you drunk today?

Are you aware of how much you should be drinking?

Before you worry that we are about to go into a diet booklet, I reassure you this is not the case. But it is a reminder that self-care at its most basic level is making sure we are fed and watered.

We make choices every time we put something in our mouths. All I am suggesting is that this humble chocolate acts as a nudge to raise your awareness.

If you decide to take things further and make changes to your diet, get advice, from a nutritionist or your GP.

There are also many magazines and online and available in print offering advice and recipes. You might be someone who likes to have an accountability buddy. This could be by joining one of the clubs set up to help you lose weight or using an app or just telling someone who'll check in with you.

The lovely coconut is a reminder to eat fresh fruit and vegetables. The World Heath Organisation and the National Health Service both recommend 5 portions a day. The NHS website has tips on how to include 5 a day into our diets.

There are so many recipe books to choose from, I am not going to recommend any particular here. But I do recommend cooking one of your favourite meals as a form of self care.

Not only are you getting the enjoyment from preparing and cooking the meal, but the reward of eating it. Take your time when eating, savour every mouthful. So often these days we are in a rush or watching television while eating. Then there is the times we are looking after someone else whilst trying to eat ourselves.

Take your time, savor every mouthful.

I would just like to mention that chocolate itself is a very good ingrediant used in both savoury and sweet dishes. For example chocolate is often used in chilli, as well as mole sauce and with venison. Did you know white chocolate sauce goes with salmon? Chocolate is in many deserts including chocolate mousse, chocolate fondant and my favourite chocolate cake. Preferably baked by my mum. Now I know that is not available to you, but I bet you have a favourite chocolate related dish. I'm sure you can name many more dishes.

Remember the coconut water, we all need to keep hydrated to maintain our wellbeing. I know it is not often talked about, but do you know the colour of your pee. This is one way you can tell if you are hydrated enough. In case you are not sure it should be a light colour.

Why am I talking about this, well you will not be surprised to know that being dehydrated can effect your health. Do you reach for food when really you need a drink of water. Or are you feeling tired, maybe you need to rehydrate. So keep taking the sips throughout the day.

Now let me get back to eating the lovely Coconut Chocolate Truffle, which does not count as one of my five a day, but does taste good.

Make a note of your thoughts.

_____

_____

_____

_____

_____

_____

Use this space to be creative; Doodle, Mindmap, or Draw.

TIME TO FILL YOUR OWN CHOC-O-CARE BOX

That's it the chocolate box is empty, the wrappers have been thrown away, but before you throw the box away let's think about you and which chocolate you will put in your box, which self-care activity you are going to do.

If you're anything like me you can eat a box of chocolates almost unconsciously, somehow your hand reaches out before you have engaged your mind. Now I know that it is not good for us to eat a box in one sitting, all that sugar whizzing round body could do untold damage. If we fill the chocolate box back up with our self-care choc-o-care activities, we will have miraculously turned the chocolate box into a Choc-o-Care box full of goodies.

They will help us to feel happier, be healthier, and improve our physical and mental wellbeing. That's got to be a good thing surely.

Yes, I can hear some of you saying that would be great to feel like that, but some of you are still saying to yourself "yes, but I can't/won't". Others are just thinking "No way."

Imagine this guide to the chocolate box. It's found either underneath the box, on the inside lid or a card inside the box.

We can spend hours reading all the descriptions of the individual chocolates before making our very deliberate choice. Sometimes we might just pick one and then ask "what's this".

Looking at the following guide, or reading through the individual descriptions above, select three chocolates to get you started.

Chocolate	Focus area- PMES	Action
Nutty Caramel	P	Exercise
Honeycombe Batton	P,M,E,S	Being Outdoors
Creamy Fudge	P,M,E,S	Unplug & relax
Turkish Delight	E	Social Connection
Praline	E,M,S	Laughter
Toffee Baton	M	Puzzle Games
Gooey Caramel	M, S	Mindfulness Meditation
Orange Crisp	P, E	Music, Dance, Move
Strawberry Cream	E, S	Being thankful
Coffee Cream	M, E	Your support group
Coconut Truffle	P,M,E	Eating & Drinking

YOUR SELECTION.

Write the name of your chocolate in the box.

Choc-o-Care 1   Choc-o-Care 2   Choc-o-Care 3

Now think about the activity or action that you are going to do.

You are more likely to do it if you make a commitment yourself to do it.

This is a very important moment, think through your WHY's, this helps to write your INTENTION. Look at the notes you have made as you have read the book.

For each Choc o Care chosen;

First name your Choc-o-Care activity or action.

Setting your intention.

_____

_____

_____

_____

_____

Second make an appointment – what time and date, write it down, put it in your online diary, put it on your home calendar. We are more likely to keep an appointment if we have planned the time and where the activity/action occurs.

_____

_____

_____

_____

_____

Third – how much time you are giving it, which is really, how much time you are giving yourself. So how long are you going to make the appointment?

_____

_____

_____

_____

_____

Committing is like promising yourself that you are prepared to nurture yourself, to make your OWN self-care a priority.

Complete the Declaration on the next page, pin a copy where you will see it, and make it a screen saver.

The Declaration

I promise to take care of myself, to nurture myself, to make me a priority.

1) I am going to (activity/action)_____

when (day/date)_____ at (time)_____

for how long_____

2) I am going to (activity/action)_____

when (day/date)_____ at (time)_____

for how long_____

3) I am going to (activity/action)_____

when (day/date)_____ at (time)_____

for how long_____

THE EMERGENCY PACK
OF CHOC-O-CARE

If you are still not convinced that you can spend any time on self-care, or looking after yourself, then begin by just taking 5 minutes at a time.

I know that's longer than it takes to eat one chocolate. But it's just 15 minutes on the first day to eat three chocolates, can you do that?

Yes you can; you have got this far because you know that you want to be that person who look after their own wellbeing.

So commit to sampling the following chocolates today:

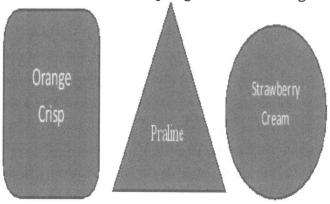

EMERGENCY PACK INSTRUCTIONS

Orange Crisp

I am going to (activity/action) _play music and dance_

when (day/date)_today_ at (time)_12:30_ for how long _5 minutes_

Praline

I am going to (activity/action) _watch a funny YouTube clip and laugh_ when _today_ for how long _5 minutes_

Strawberry Cream

I am going to (activity/action) _write a gratitude list, ten things I am grateful for_ when _today_ for how long _5 minutes_

Repeat this the next day, and the next day, increasing the time to 10 minutes a day. Before long you'll be making up your own box of choc o care.

We never know what circumstances will cause us to need to call on the Emergency Pack of Choc-o-Care. It could be that we are short of time, there is an emergancy at home or at work, your routines are disrupted or you are just not feeling great.

Make sure you have prepared your emergency pack, have it close to hand.

When needed....

Sit down and have a chocolate.....what would be your go to chocolate? Just take 5 to STOP, take a BREATH and release the tension, gently roll your shoulders, whilst eating your chocolate.

Always remember to refill the emergency pack!

STILL STRUGGLING TO THINK OF SELF CARE ACTIVITIES

Here are are a few ideas to get you thinking:

1) Watch the clouds.

2) Water your plants.

3) Dress up for dinner.

4) Stroke your pet.

5) Give a surprise gift to a friend or family member.

6) Go on a treasure hunt - find 5 new things or objects in your immediate environment.

7) Call the first person in your phone book who you have not spoken to in the last month.

8) Sit on the grass.

9) Watch your favourite childhood movie.

10) Note down 3 things you have done well today.

11) Smile at yourself in the mirror.

12) Have a good laugh.

13) Drink plenty of water - stay hydrated.

14) Treat yourself, we all need a treat sometimes.

15) Pay a compliment to the next person you meet.

16) Have a siesta.

17) Stretch out, be like a cat.

18) Do 20 star jumps.

19) Sing in the car.

20) Tell a joke.

21) Write out an affirmation.

22) Read a poem.

23) Make a collage.

24) Keep a journal.

25) Buy yourself flowers.

26) Turn off your phone.

27) Volunteer.

28) Paint.

29) Try Yoga.

30) Go for a walk.

31) Have an early night.

32) Write a letter to a friend.

35) Play some music...loudly and dance.

36) Take up Knitting.

37) Go for a swim

38) Take up cold water swimming if you dare.

39) Put something on your workstation/desk that will make you smile

40) Plant some bulbs

41) Meditate

42) Try an exercise class you have never taken before

43) Sip a delicious mug of chocolate

45) Moisturise your hands

47) Display a photograph you love in a frame

48) Be still, listen what can you hear all around you.

49) Have a hug

50) Create your Choc-o-care box of chocolates

Keep adding to this list, remember they do not have to be big and expensive things, small is good. The key is to make the activity a habit.

_____
_____
_____
_____
_____
_____
_____
_____
_____
_____
_____
_____
_____
_____
_____
_____
_____
_____

Use this space to be creative; Doodle, Mind Map or Draw your thoughts and ideas.

AND NOW

We all know what a box of chocolates is and for most of us without underlying health problems we do not have any trouble eating them. Sometimes we might saviour one more than others, sometimes we share with others and sometimes someone is sharing with us. We do not have to be taught how to take one and eat it; we have that nailed.

I would love it,if you are reminded to check in on your OWN wellbeing the next time you eat chocolate.

How are you?

Can you describe your mood?

Do a body scan. Can you feel any tension anywhere?

How WELL are YOU taking care of YOURSELF?

Then to feel inspired to take action..go on, go for it.

Let me know what you fill your choc-o-care box of chocolates with.

Having a chocolate will never be the same again, and it might just help you LOOK AFTER YOURSELF.

AN INVITATION FROM THE AUTHOR

Writing this book has been part of my own self care journey. It has allowed me to look at my own daily practises.

Over the years I have acquired and practiced many tools and techniques, as a life coach, speaker and trainer. Bringing some of these together in this book has given me great pleasure and a good excuse to eat chocolates.

I hope that you are feeling inspired to fill your choc-o-care box and start your own journey.

I would love to hear how you are getting on, email me on anne@awayforward.com

If you would like to discuss coaching contact me on:

http://www.awayforwardcoaching.com

DO YOU KNOW.....

In the USA the National Confectioners Association recognise the 19th February as Chocolate Mint Day.

BONUS CHOCOLATE

An extra chocolate for you to consider as part of your choco-o-box of self care choc's.

CHOCOLATE MINT (M,E,S)

This is a bonus chocolate, like the one served at the end of a meal. Is it a digestive or is it a pure indulgence?

The taste can certainly make your tongue tingle, the fresh minty mingles with the bitter dark chocolate flavour. Often its a peppermint fondant filling but sometimes it's a solid chocolate with what feel like shards of mint running through it. I personally like them all.

One particular brand that comes to mind when I take a moment to consider the chocolate mint, and for me they are associated with Christmas. As I remember it, they were only in our house at this time of year. They were a special chocolate for the adults....but maybe that is just my memory playing tricks!

One of the key ingredients of a chocolate mint is peppermint oil, this is a natural oil extracted from the leaves of the plant. Peppermint oil is an essential oil used in aromotherapy. When we think of different ways of self care, for some people using aromotherapy oils is something they will incorpaorate into their self care regime.

Aromotherapy oils have been used in numerous ways dating back centuaries, to 3500BC. Historians have found evidence of there use in Asia, Ancient Egypt and the around the Mediterranean. The International Federation of Aromotherapist website has a more detailed history if you are interested.

But for now, I will just add that the oils can be added to a massage oil or used in a diffuser. It is best to get advice from a qualified person before using them. Peppermint oil is often used as a digestive aid and to help alleviate headaches.

Chocolate mint is also a plant, the *Mentha x piperita*. It is a member of the mint family, *Lamiaceae*. It is a herb you can grow and use in your cooking. This brings together several self care activities, connecting with nature, mindfulness, and nourishing the body.

A chocolate mint plant can be grown in your garden or if you have little space in a container. Take time to nurture it, watching it grow.

Get your senses engaged.

Look at the colour of the leaves, what different tones can you see. Are they changing colour with the seasons?

What texture do the leaves have? Brush your fingers gently over them. What does the leaf feel like? Is it rough, smooth, is it hairy? Does the top and the underside feel the same or are they different?

Can you smell the chocolaty aroma? does the leaf need to be rubbed between your fingers before you can smell it?

What does it taste like as you crush a leaf in your mouth? Is there an explosion of minty freshness, can you taste the chocolate?

Use it as an infusion, with hot water. Take your time to sip, sit back and relax.

You can use other edible herbs to do the exercise above and it is a way of engaging your senses with the natural world.

All this from the humble chocolate mint. A chocolate that can so easily be over looked!

make a note of your thoughts

_____
_____
_____

Use this space to be creative; Doodle, Mindmap or Draw your thoughts and ideas.

That is all the chocolates that I have put in my choc-o-care box. There are many more chocolates, if I have not considered one of your favourites then go ahead and include it in your choc-o-care box

Just think about the flavour and texture.

What is the taste, is it a nutty, hard or soft centred chocolate?

_____
_____
_____
_____

then

What does does it remind you of? Is it a place, sensation, child-hood?

_____
_____
_____

How can you caputure this with a self care activity?

_____
_____
_____

that's all there is to it!!!

TAKE A CHOCO BREAK WITH THIS WORD SEARCH

```
S  O  C  I  A  L  J  T  H  G  U  L  P  N  U
T  E  X  E  R  C  I  S  E  W  Y  H  U  C  E
M  B  L  A  Y  Z  D  C  A  C  A  O  Z  L  C
A  D  T  F  A  N  E  S  V  J  T  M  Z  C  O
E  C  H  O  C  O  L  A  T  E  H  O  L  S  M
F  H  A  U  H  A  E  I  W  B  A  U  E  I  X
P  O  D  X  M  F  R  U  O  B  N  T  N  D  B
L  C  O  C  O  A  Q  E  O  T  K  D  R  M  C
H  O  S  G  V  G  P  X  P  I  F  O  T  U  S
I  C  D  T  E  C  R  O  S  U  U  O  V  S  U
L  A  U  G  H  T  E  R  L  G  L  R  E  I  G
O  R  P  S  Q  L  O  N  Y  A  L  S  K  C  A
S  E  Y  I  B  H  E  D  V  C  N  X  A  Q  R
D  A  N  C  E  S  K  C  B  R  E  A  T  H  E
C  G  K  E  S  E  L  E  C  T  I  O  N  Z  T
```

3 letter	4 letter	5 letter	6 letter	7 letter
BOX	MOVE	SUGAR	UNPLUG	BREATHE
POD	COCOA	PUZZLE		
	CACAO	SOCIAL		
	MUSIC			
	DANCE			

8 letter	9 letter	11 letter
SELFCARE	CHOCOCARE	MINDFULNESS
LAUGHTER	SELECTION	
THANKFUL	CHOCOLATE	
EXERCISE		
OUTDOORS		

The words below are all associated with chocolate. Can you unscramble them to reveal them.

IAMSORASEMER   ----------------------------------

KILM   ----------------------------------

NYOFRITECNOA   ----------------------------------

OSTNECILE   ----------------------------------

TIWHE   ----------------------------------

DFUGE   ----------------------------------

ACBACNAEO   ----------------------------------

NAIPELR   ----------------------------------

LXRAE   ----------------------------------

Make a list of all the different chocolates you have eaten, starting as a child. How many of them are still available?

Can you remember the wrappers, have a go at drawing some of them?
What colour where/are they?
What is the lettering like?

Do you remember any of the advertising slogans?

ACKNOWLEDGEMENT

I have had the support and encouragement from many friends and family during this writing process.

A special thank you to Sarah Males who was there at the inception of the idea. Carol Higgins, Izzy Davies and Jackie Goodridrige for spending time reading drafts and giving feedback. Shelagh Fisher for the tasty home made chocolates featured in the photographs. Dawn Ardagh, thank you for all of this and more, your encouragement helped me to finish this book.

Over the years I have been on many courses and attended worshops all of which have inspired me and helped me. I am grateful for to Animas Centre for Coaching, where I trained and gained a Diploma in Transformational Coaching.

ABOUT THE AUTHOR

Anne Goodridge

Anne Goodridge is a qualified life coach and public speaker. She enjoys delivering workshops on self care and personal development and has worked many years as a Social Worker. To relax she enjoys being outdoors and loves walking. She achieved one of her dreams when she walked the Camino de Santiago. Anne enjoys fun and laughter and seeks to include this in her work.

A PICK AND MIX OF A FEW
INTERESTING THINGS

I Have Read While Writing

Charlie and the Chocolate Factory - Roald Dahl
loved this book as a child and have happy memories of watching
the film

Around the World in 80 Days - Jules Verne
Again a childhood memory

Where the Wild Winds Are - Nick Hunt
This book allowed me to travel when I had to *stay home*.

Marley & Me - John Grogan
I loved this book following the adventures of Marley and the Grogan family.

The Bees - Carol Ann Duffy
A beautiful collection of poems.

The Energy Bus - John Gordon
What a ride, a fable with insights in how to live life.

Between the Stops - Sany Toksvig
I lived in London for a number of years and have been a passenger
on this book, a great read.

Tuesdays with Morrie - Mitch Albom
A book passed to me by a friend, insightful and memorable.

The Old Ways - Robert Macfalane
Brings nature to life, I was wandering on the Old Ways as I read.

The Salt Path - Raynor Winn
I was walking every step of the way with Raynor and her husband.

Psychologies magazine
Country Walking Magazine

Websites I Visited While Writing

www.bbc.co.uk/sounds:
Ramblings and Desert Island Discs,
Your Dead to Me: The History of Chocolate

www.henpicked.net - for women over 40 sharing articles and tips
on happiness, health, wealth and menopause

www.happify.com - builds skills for lasting happiness

www.nature.com - a scientific journal of peer reviewed research
in science, technology and natural sciences.

Chocolates I Have Eaten While Writing

Far too numerous to mention. Lets just say that I have taken the
research extremely seriously!!

Extra space to Doodle, mind map or draw your own choc-o-care box of chocolates

Extra space to Doodle, Mind Map, Draw your own Emergency Choc-o-care box

THE DECLARATION

I promise to take care of myself, to nurture myself, to make me a priority.

1) I am going to
(activity/action)_____
when(day/date)_____at_____(time)
for how long_____

2) I am going to
(activity/action)_____
when(day/date)_____at_____(time)
for how long_____

3) I am going to
(activity/action)_____
when(day/action)_____at_____ (time)
for how long_____

THANK YOU FOR READING THIS BOOK, ENJOY YOUR CHOCOLATES

Printed in Great Britain
by Amazon